Diary of a
(usually)
Quite Contented Cat

Dedicated to my grandson James,
who features in this story as a cute little bub!

© Pia Horan-Gross, 2018

All rights reserved. No portion of this book may be reproduced, stored in a retrieval system, or transmitted in any form or by any means – electronic, mechanical, photocopy, recording, scanning, or other – except for brief quotations in critical reviews or articles, without the prior written permission by the author/self-publisher.

ISBN 978-0-6480135-5-6

Diary of a
(usually)
Quite Contented Cat

Written by
Pia Horan-Gross
(Sprinkled with lots of laughter)

ALSO BY PIA HORAN-GROSS:

*The Puppy Who Wouldn't Share

*My Best Poems - Complete Collection

*My Best Poems, Part 1 - Celebrating Nature

*My Best Poems, Part 2 - The Challenge of Relationships

*My Best Poems, Part 3 - Spirituality, The Pathos of the Heart and the Triumph of the Spirit

Introduction

Cats have always featured prominently in our mini family, consisting then of Becky, my youngest daughter, Sara her older sister and me, a struggling single mother. We acquired our first cat Charly in Lismore, in rural Australia, a "tiger" cat, who later, when moving back to Sydney, became our valiant knight and protector. He took his role very seriously and fought off brown snakes (a nest in our garden), wild tomcats coming in at night from the adjacent bush and even dogs, who considered our then unfenced property "free for all" – until they met Charly!!

Charly was strictly Sara's cat but cats choose their own favourites and so he spent much time on Bec's lap, while she was doing her homework in her room.

Along came Annie, whom the then teenage girls called "Annie Bunny", "Anybody", "Annbun" for short or, if lucky, Annie! She was a little cute, longsuffering, black and white, very soft and cuddly lamb of a cat. So much so, the girls used to carry her wrapped around their necks, like in the picture of Jesus the Shepherd, carrying the lost lamb.

Both cats have now long gone, buried in separate plots in our garden, where they loved to sun themselves, especially in the mild winter's sun.

After the girls left home, Ron (my ex-husband) moved in and with him a whirlwind of cats; stray cats, pregnant cats, old cats and kittens. I had never experienced anything like it but it was truly breathtaking!

My present hesitation to invite another cat to live with me, now a grandmother, must be due to the fact that I never fully recovered from a condition commonly called "post traumatic furniture destruction syndrome"!

The story in this book centers around a cat called Ginseng or Ginsy for short. He was part of a litter of four, born in our house from a very lean, dark grey stray mother cat, which Ron adopted, shortly after we got married. This cat had peculiar habits, such as getting up on the highest point of cupboards and spending the day sleeping there.

She obviously had previously experienced a threatening environment and therefore went for the safest spot she could find.

Her litter consisted of a turtle shell cat, a grey cat and two ginger and white cats. When older, we would watch them playing together, chasing each other round and round the same obstacle courses, including book shelves, lounges, under beds – you name it!

Eventually, we needed to find new owners for three of them; always a sad but necessary task, if we (read "I") wanted to keep control of our home!

Ginseng was the luckiest of them, for he enjoyed his mother's affection the longest!

Nevertheless, there was a streak of wildness in him and relatives and friends, even us, would at times be on the receiving end of his sudden nips or swipes, which we strongly tried to discourage. We believe that the father would have been a tomcat, a ginger one.

We managed to "tame him" sufficiently to become a rather pleasant and endearing pet, using such means as a water spray bottle, time out in the "Study" (at times, he would take himself there when having been naughty!) and determined "no's"!

Here then, is a book summary of the things he would get up to, in condensed diary form! I originally wrote this account while suffering a particularly nasty and prolonged flu virus, during winter of 2004. The original has been edited for publication, photos and my own drawings replaced with professional illustrations.

May you enjoy an extract from the life of a truly funny and endearing cat named Ginseng, also called Ginsy, a cat with personality plus!

P.H-G

Contents

Introduction		v
Sunday, 6 June	**THIS IS ME!**	1
Monday, 7 June	**LAP TIME**	7
Tuesday, 8 June	**STUCK ON TOP OF A TREE**	9
Wednesday, 9 June	**A RECURRING NIGHTMARE**	12
Thursday, 10 June	**PLAY STYLES**	14
Friday, 11 June	**THE GOOD AND THE BAD!**	16
Saturday, 12 June	**RUDE INTRUSIONS AND OTHER ANNOYANCES**	18
Wednesday, 16 June	**AM: JAMES VISITING**	20
Thursday, 17 June	**FORGIVEN!**	22
Friday, 25 June	**BARRED!**	24
Sunday, 26 June	**DAD MISBEHAVING**	25
Wednesday, 30 June	**AN UNNERVING LITTLE BRAT BUT CUTE!**	26
Monday, 5 July	**THE INTRUDER IN THE MIDDLE OF THE NIGHT**	29
Thursday, 8 July	**HEATERS AND WARM BEVERAGES**	31
Tuesday, 13 July	**COMINGS AND GOINGS IN OUR HOUSE**	33
Saturday, 24 July	**JUST LIKE A FILM STAR!**	34
Sunday, 25 July	**BEDS, BEDS, BEDS!**	35

Saturday, 31 July	**CAT BLISS**	39
Saturday, 14 August	**CHECKMATE!**	40
Tuesday, 24 August	**A MISSED OPPORTUNITY**	42
Wednesday, 2 September	**BETRAYAL AND MOVING ON TO A SECRET DIARY**	43

Diary of a (usually) Quite Contented Cat

Sunday, 6 June **THIS IS ME!**

Today is a crisp, sunny winter's morning in Sydney, Australia.

My name is Ginseng, or "Ginsy" for short, which apparently means Ginger, because of my ginger and white coloured coat. Makes sense, I think.

I live in an outer suburb of this city, surrounded by bush (a Wildlife Nature Park), with a storm water creek running alongside the lower part of our property.

Neighbouring cats and dogs think it's a really fun place to come and explore- but I won't have it! It's my contribution here; to keep riff raff out of this place!

Sometimes, we get funny hopping giants called "wallabies" in our garden. My mum and dad don't like them much because they chew up lots of plants, especially newly planted ones!

As well, there are some hideous and scary birds that come into the garden. They have a weird red neck, with enormous hind legs and scary talons. They make a big mess, especially with newly mulched garden beds which they spread everywhere!

They make drum-like sounds and seem to mutter like old men.

Mum discovered nine of them one morning and pelted them with onions, potatoes, rocks…gee she was very annoyed! They always come back, as if nothing happened. "Infuriating", mum says!

I have done my morning garden inspection, sunned for a while on a comfy bed of leaves, until the neighbour bullies (two teenage girls) start yelling at me across the fence, telling their dog to pretend he is going to eat me for breakfast!

My dad says that they are best left alone, so I hurry to leave my sunny spot and run down to the house. Dad is waiting for me, he has heard the commotion.

I have a "friend" called "Zippy", who lives at the top of our place, in a neighbouring house. When I say top, I mean at the top of our land, not our house, of course.

She says I shouldn't call my owner "dad", that only cats can be dads and mums. Dad says that he is my dad and that mum is my mum. Kind of being adopted or something.

That's fine with me, except that lately I would rather be their grandson, because of all the fuss being made of the latest family member on the scene – a little brat called James!

They treat him like the very sun is shining out of his gappy mouth! What **really** comes out of his mouth is a lot of ear piercing noises! If I carried on like that when I am hungry, I'd never hear the end of it! Instead, I get shoved aside; apparently I am not hygienic enough, or something along those lines. What baloney, do they wash five or six times a day?

Of course not!

I think the whole thing stinks and when he arrives on the scene, I leave in disgust and go next door, where the divine Becky lives. But more about her later.

Getting back to Zippy, my neighbour's cat; she is only "sort of a friend" because, the other day, she dared coming down to the house, wanting pats from mum and dad. I was not impressed and when I told Zippy to "scram", she had the audacity to object. We had quite a yelling match, till mum came out and Zippy suddenly felt guilty and took off! I don't like so-called friends who take liberties! Pats are best kept in one's own home and not sought willy-nilly.

Presently, I am lying on mum and dad's large bed, with the sun shining in. Mum is sick in bed. She has been for days and days. Some flu, they say. She talks funny and coughs funny. I jump up on her bed every morning and can tell straightaway if she is any better. It's the eyes that give her away. They look weary. The best I can do is to keep her company for now.

It's late afternoon now and neighbours (near Zippy's place) have come down to the bottom of their garden, at the same level where our house is. They are a stone throw from us and we can hear every word they are saying, as well as chattering by kids.

There are two kids and a dad and their pesky dog called "Frisky". Today, he behaves as if he owns the place!

Usually, he keeps a safe distance from me, and I can come and go into his area of the garden, without him doing anything about it. That proves to me that cats are much better watch cats than dogs are! But when his family is with him, he thinks he has to pretend to be "Scooby Do" or something!

I can see him now, through the lacy curtains, strutting into our garden and behaving as if the place belongs to him. It just galls me! If I wasn't so comfy and mum wasn't in need of company, I swear, I'd send him packing!

Monday, 7 June **LAP TIME**

Mum's flu is still keeping her rugged up in her off-white winter morning gown, black ugh boots, fluorescent pink thick woollen socks, her red and white polka dotted flannelette nightie, blue knitted scarf (usually dad wears it but he doesn't mind, especially when she is sick) and a wine-coloured beanie. The reason for such an extraordinarily large amount of "pelts", as I call them, inside the house is that, according to dad, the house is an ice chest in winter.

his is due to the large amount of trees surrounding the house and keeping the winter sun away. The effect of this is that everyone huddles around the heater in the lounge room, near the TV, including occasional guests. That means that mum and dad sit a lot, watching tele. For me, it means lots of lap time, gentle stroking, softly spoken little nothings – **heaven!**

Today, mum sat for three hours and during the day! What a bonus! She was watching "A Big Country", with her favourite movie star: Gregory Peck!

I think it must be for her like for me watching a mouse poking out its head before venturing out of its nest, just before I make the strategic move, I never get sick of it!

Mum says she has seen "A Big Country" at least fifteen times already, but she still rewinds the DVD when someone interrupts.

I could have sat there all day, but then she said she felt exhausted, put me down, switched off the heater and went to bed. Even though she didn't have to catch a mouse…

Tuesday, 8 June **STUCK ON TOP OF A TREE**

Today, mum is sitting outside in the sun, on some cushions, near the front steps. She wears her usual "pelts", except that she has added a pair of flannel pajamas as well, just in case. She has a blanket wrapped around her.

It's another sunny, cool day and the birds are making a racket! People tend to think that bird sounds are pretty or something. All I can hear is a bunch of minors arguing amongst themselves which one chased away the most birds in the garden. Sometimes, they flock to the top of our tall palm tree, at the back of our house. Then, when

I walk past underneath, they start heckling me: "Ginger winger! Ginger winger!" And on and on they go! If only I could put my claws around their skinny necks!

But back to mum. First, I try to cheer her up by pretending I am a hunter chasing all sorts of things, playing "tiger, tiger in the grass" and chasing birds up in the trees - it works every time!

I run up this tall Casuarina tree outside the front of our house (one of many), Casuarinas have nice rough bark to climb on. Oops! I got a bit carried away and feel a little giddy when I look down!

Mum laughs and calls "Ron!" in her croaky voice (that's my dad's name). He is pottering in the kitchen and thinks:"When can I finally start fixing my fishing rod?" But he says nothing and comes out to see what's happening. I can tell, he feels real proud to see me up there! He makes this funny whistling sound that means "it's play time!" I get kind of wild and crazy and mum laughs even more.

It's a little later in the morning. I hear dad talking to our neighbour Harry, who lives next to Zippy's place. Harry is quite old, a widower who potters a lot in his shed. He likes his chats with dad. Men-kind of talk about fishing, mates, car and boat engines, you name it. Sometimes, he tells dad how lonely he feels since his wife passed away. I sometimes go and listen to them.

Harry's place is near one of my sunny, leafy spots, with shady ferns nearby for protection from summer heat. I might as well check things out up there…

Wednesday, 9 June **A RECURRING NIGHTMARE**

Mum got up early today – she wanted to water the garden at the front of the house. Mum says that we haven't had decent rain for years. People are only allowed to use the sprinklers on certain days and times. Today is one of those days. Mum says the garden looks as dry as she feels inside because of the "swallowing thing". If she tries to drink, it comes back out through her nose. I know, because she even dripped on me the other day!

Today, dad has decided to go fishing. He's been talking about it for days but was worried about leaving mum. Mum and dad went to see the doctor yesterday and she got some more medicines. She says that she can swallow better and is starting to take some solids. I think, if she had some of my dried cat food, it wouldn't go down yet. Probably, my tinned food she might manage, as long as it was made sloppy.

I could tell, she felt happy for dad to go fishing – the "nice kind" of happiness. That means, I have to be man about the house till he gets back!

Now, I am lying near the heater, mum is sitting in the lounge chair, next to me. The house is quiet, the birds outside- reasonable! I feel heavier and heavier and heavier...

Now, I am outside, stalking the bushes for rats, mice and anything of interest. But what's that? Oh no! Not the sticky, stinging flies again! Quick, run or they get in my

fur and sting like crazy! I can't move! They are coming! Help! Dad! Mum! I wake up with a start – phew! It was only a dream. I am safe. No sticky flies.
Ah! Blissful warmth!

Thursday, 10 June **PLAY STYLES**

Last night was great fun! Becky came over and sat in her usual lounge chair, near me. There's a chair for mum, just opposite the TV (she says it's best for her neck), then there's the lounge, where dad usually lies, and the third lounge chair; for Becky or visitors. The heater is usually closest to that chair and I usually lie in front of it, enjoying the peace and warmth.

When Becky arrived, she exclaimed: "Gin-seee", with the "seee" going high pitch. To me that means: "There you are, little fellow, let's play!"

When mum wants to play, she usually looks at me and, all of a sudden, she makes these goggly eyes at me. That too means: "Let's play!"

Dad just does his funny whistle sound.

Anyway, last night it was Becky's turn. I usually start off by turning over onto my back and playing dead, while getting ready to pounce! Sure enough, soon I feel her gentle finger tips on my belly. Ooooh! It's so hard trying to resist going for her hands! I usually can't help it. And she knows!

Nevertheless, I go on playing dead, waiting for the strategic moment. So she pokes me a bit more, laughing wickedly. Her dark brown eyes get very big and all her teeth are showing! NOW! I make a move… but she was ready! Start again! It's great fun!

Today, the weather has changed to dull grey. Everyone is holding their breath – it could finally rain! All I want to do is sleep near the heater.

The day ended with just a few drops of rain, I felt them because I had shifted to a comfy chair, outside on the veranda.

Back near the heater now. Dad says we only had a spit of rain, that's all!

Friday, 11 June **THE GOOD AND THE BAD!**

Today has been very good and very bad. Very good, because both mum and dad made time to play. First, dad with the silly toy mouse on a string and secretly tying a plastic bag on my tail to get me frantic. Mum wasn't too happy about that! She needn't have worried – I got it off in two seconds flat and got the mouse instead! What do they think, that I am still a silly kitten?!

Then mum went to make the bed and I raced into it, before she could pull the sheets back and made my crazy goggly eyes at her (like she does at me, sometimes). She says that my eyes go black when I do that. I ran very fast backwards and forwards. The real fun began when she pulled the sheets over me. Whenever she tried to tuck the sheet in, I was there in a flash and she gave a little screech. It's not a good idea to let me catch her fingers! Sometimes, she squeezes my back through the sheets. That sends me off purring and meowing, all at the same time! By the time she pulled the heavy winter doona across, I had slid out from under the sheets, at the side of the bed.

That was the good part. As well, catching some of today's meagre sun, down at "Annie's Corner", where mum and dad usually sit for a while, in winter.

Annie was a black and white cat that used to live here. She was very very old and very cranky, especially with a then kitten like me, who used her as a landing pad for surprise high altitude trapeze acts! She used to daily lie in that corner, to warm her old bones.

Now comes the bad bit. When we came back up to the house today, I had the distinct feeling that it must be close to dinner time. I tried to let mum and dad know about that. Mum says that I usually think it's dinner time shortly after breakfast. I just think that eating is almost as much fun as playing. If I could eat and play alternately, I would know that I have arrived in cat heaven!

Anyway, I hate when they ignore me, like they did this morning. So I repeated my request. After several more attempts, mum finally said "No!" in a firm voice. I know that she has said no in the past, and then changed her mind. So I tried again, rubbing against her shins, just so she wouldn't forget. Next, she lifted me up and unceremoniously (that's long for "without fuss") put me out into the cold! The humility of it! But wait! Dad wanted to come to my rescue (he understands, he hates the cold too). But I just heard mum say something about me wearing a fur coat and then the door shut, and stayed shut!

Saturday, 12 June
RUDE INTRUSIONS AND OTHER ANNOYANCES

Today, we all seemed to get up on the wrong foot. I definitely felt that breakfast was on the meagre side and I sure let them know! It did not make any difference. They ignored me, and worse, told me off and even gave me the door treatment again. My nose was out of joint all day, until just after 3 pm this avo (Aussie slang for afternoon), when lo and behold, dinner arrived early! Mum was having late lunch with Becky and I think she felt sorry for me. So she should!

Another thing that really "cheesed" me off was those pesky neighbours' boys coming down near our property, on the other side of the creek, playing cowboys and Indians, so it seemed. I was semiserenely (only "semi" because of the breakfast incident) lying near mum and dad, near Annie's Corner, enjoying the warm sunshine, when all of a sudden, I heard boys' voices, what seemed like next to me! It gave me such a shock that I bolted for our house, despite the reassuring calls from mum and dad.

The rest of the day is a brief series of clear moments of waking and a very long stretch of "comatosis" (it's one of mum's favourite terms for being a lazy blob).

One of the clear moments was, of course, dinner. Another, Becky arriving home from one of her shifts, looking after lots of human Annies. She found me in the study, near the heater, near mum. We both fled there, due to dad having card night here tonight, with three noisy friends of his.

Overall, it's been a day of rude intrusions, a meagre breakfast and, I have to add, poor consideration of basic cats' rights. One of them is to a peaceful home environment. If this keeps up, I'll have to consider taking some action. I'll sleep on it first, though…

Wednesday, 16 June **AM: JAMES VISITING**☹
PM: BOYS' NIGHT☺

I have had writer's block for the past few days, therefore no entry for some time.

Presently, it's "boys night" in the lounge room. Just the two of us sprawled on the lounge, with our favourite blanket between us; dad watching the footy and I keeping him company, mum once again fleeing the scene. Ah! Male bonding is such a lost art and we two master it to perfection! GO BULLDOGS! But what am I saying? I hate dogs!

Today, the little screaming brat was here again (you know, James, the grandson).

I overcame my past intense dislike and decided to see how that pink face of his smelled. He stared at me in disbelief and then gave me a big smile. Quite cute for a brat, I must say!

The day outside was sunny and pleasant enough to lie around in the sun, so I decided to spend the day in peace and quiet down at Annie's Corner. Dad joined me after a while and then mum came down as well, with James in her arms! **Really!?**

He kept looking at both dad and me and thought it was great fun, especially when we both decided to play dead. Dad started it first; lying down with his head on a boulder, his feet up on a chair. It looked really comfy, so I lied down on my back too, with my hind legs up against a fence post. Gee! Dad really knows about comfort. What a discovery!

Mum wanted to take a photo of us two (she said no one would believe what she saw) but then decided that one of us (probably me) would have moved by the time she ran all the way up the steps and back down again. I am sure though that this is going to be the standard posture for both of us in the future, so she will have many more opportunities to photograph us!

After a while, mum left with James and I later heard a few more screaming sessions coming from the house.

I felt safe and peaceful where I was.

The rest of the day went pretty smoothly. The usual habit of lying near the heater at night, dad on the couch watching footy, mum nowhere to be seen.

Ah well! All is well that ends well.

Thursday, 17 June **FORGIVEN!**

Miserable morning, I felt irritable and had a swipe at dad. Got put into the "naughty boy's room" (funny, that's usually where James sleeps…).

Actually, I knew what was coming, so trotted in there on my own volition. Dad gave me a lecture about proper behaviour for cats, and then the door shut. It always works: in the quiet isolation of this room, I usually arrive at a deep sense of "contrition". A new word I overheard mum use, apparently it means "feeling sorry for bad behaviour".

Later on, when dad was lying down, I went up to him and licked his scratched hand, as a peace offering. He is very forgiving and he smiled at me and patted me straightaway. Ah! The relief of being forgiven! That's when the day really started for me. I heard him say to mum that he thought I was out of sorts because of James' visit yesterday. You bet I am!

We then napped on the bed for a while, and then he got up and started mowing. I napped some more.

Later that night we had some visitors: Becky and her friend Tony. I was lying near the heater, as usual. Tony likes cats and gave me some nice pats and let me romp with his hand. I pretend that I am a ferocious tiger, about to devour his entire hand and the secret is not to pull back. He played the game well and I let him eventually go. We played the pretend dead game, the rub my back game, especially where I have some sticky fur bits.

It always unnerves me because it feels like the sticky flies are back. That makes my fur ripple and I get quite edgy. Dad said today that he would cut the sticky fur bit off. I hope he'll do it soon!

As mum very firmly told me that the kitchen was "closed for business", I might as well snuggle down on my blanket and turn in for the night…

Friday, 25 June **BARRED!**

It's been hectic here lately! People coming and going and sleeping willy-nilly everywhere, even in mum and dad's bed! I have never seen anything like it! I was even barred from going into mum and dad's bedroom; apparently I represent a health danger for mum and dad's friend Marcel, who is an asthma sufferer! Don't talk to me about being a scapegoat- I am the arch scapegoat! The only good thing to come out of this was that dad and I slept in the lounge room.

Some good bits this week were plenty of naps (eventually) on mum and dad's bed, once things settled down. I also spent a fair bit of time napping outside in my leafy sunny spots. Dad sat with me every day down in Annie's corner. Mum sometimes joined us too. She doesn't like too much sun, as she says, it gives her freckles. I wish she had more freckles, then we would look more alike!

One morning while playing, dad tried again to tie a rope to my tail. It was off quicker than you can say "cuckoo clock"! Some people are just plain slow learners!

Sunday, 26 June **DAD MISBEHAVING**

Great day! What a start! Mum and dad played the bed game (with me, of course). Then it was off into the bathtub (it was empty), while mum was painting her face. I ducked, like when I play tiger in the grass. She threw a soft, fluffy bathmat over me. When I peeked out with just one eye, she called dad to come and see. Wanting to know what was going on, he joined us and then did a very rude and scary thing: he turned on the cold water tap! My worst nightmare! That was the end of fun and I was out of there in a flash! I heard mum scolding dad and him laughing loudly.

Apart from that, dad did behave himself quite well for the rest of the day.

Wednesday, 30 June
AN UNNERVING LITTLE BRAT BUT CUTE!

Today, I was dozing peacefully on a soft lounge chair on the veranda of Becky's cabin, which is just next to the main house. It's a bit messy, with chairs, paint canvasses, a movable trolley with bits and pieces on it and you can steal away here and not be noticed. That's what I thought, anyway. Until mum arrived with baby James in her arms, looking for me. Oh dear! She knew exactly where to find me! So I jumped off my chair, at least to say hello to mum. It's only courtesy.

I got lots of pats from mum and James grinned at me. Apparently, he had been a bit grizzly. Ginseng to the rescue, so it seemed! It did the trick.

Mum though went a bit far and put James down on the ground, to pat me, or something. I wasn't so comfortable about that! He looked mesmerized and I could feel his little hands on my tail. We both weren't quite sure what to do.

Mum's reassuring pats helped though.

After a while, I decided to do a survey of the garden and took off. Mum took James for a sightseeing tour around the garden. Two noisy kookaburras were making a racket in the trees and James looked up, to see where the noise was coming from. Mum tried to move closer to the birds but they were very high up in the tall trees.

She then sat down on the wooden bench dad built. I decided to join them. Mum put James down and this time he decided to crawl towards me, where I was sitting. The little bugger came straight for me, grinning widely. It scared me and I ran away. Unnerving, the little brat! Best kept at a distance, I say.

Later on, I heard him in the house. I decided to go and see what was going on. Mum was trying to feed him from a bottle; he was so half-hearted about it, it took mum 45 minutes to get him to drink two thirds. He wiggled and wriggled, he grizzled and drizzled and mum still laughed after all that! I wouldn't last 5 minutes and out into the cold or in the naughty boy's room I'd go! There is no justice in this world, I've always known!

Things are back to normal now. Sanity prevails once again!

Monday, 5 July
THE INTRUDER IN THE MIDDLE OF THE NIGHT

Last night, dad slept in the lounge room again, on his camping bed. I knew something was amiss because the previous afternoon mum had been packing her bags! I always know something is brewing when the suitcase comes out. I was waiting for dad to put on the footy but not so! I finally settled down, puzzled but enjoying having a sleep with my dad, knowing that some things were too mysterious even for cats to understand. And we are pretty smart when it comes to mysteries. An inborn knack some might say. But wait till you hear the rest!

In the middle of a wonderfully warm and peaceful sleep, suddenly, heavy footsteps coming up the steps and then outside, on the veranda, which woke us up! Next, a glaring torchlight shone right into our eyes and, oh shock and horror! The sliding door opened and a strange man walked in, booming loudly: "What's for breakfast?" It was pitch black outside, I thought we had a maniac on our hands!

Dad wasn't scared at all; he got up and started cooking breakfast. At least, I got breakfast too, once recovered. I then was allowed to go and play tiger in the dark, outside. When I came back, driven by the cold and hanging out for the warmth of the heater, there was a smell of coffee, burnt toast and bacon in the room. Two happy blokes, rugged in blankets, were sitting up, watching the soccer final.

I tried to settle down near the heater, which was short-lived. I kept leaping up in fright every time Peter, the noisy intruder jumped up, shouting! What a Neanderthal!

I have always thought that one should watch one's manners in other people's and cats' places; this bloke Peter obviously thought this was his place! I just wished mum had been here, she would have sorted him out!

She did return in the afternoon. When she unpacked her suitcase, I jumped in. It was an overnight bag and I fitted in just nice and snugly. Next time, I'll hide in it and see where she goes…I don't want to hang around noisy, screaming blokes again!

Thursday, 8 July
HEATERS AND WARM BEVERAGES

Something is going on in our place and it's making me nervous. Dad is endlessly packing. The lounge room, which mum likes to have looking neat and tidy, is presently in shambles! The table and chairs, even lounge chairs, are full of plastic bottles, little and largish containers, parkers, sleeping bag, rolled sleeping mat, jumpers, a huge back pack and on and on it goes.

This started a few days ago. Today, I really got the jitters!

I saw mum's suitcase (the one I just fit into) back on the bed, in the spare bedroom. Don't tell me; they are leaving again!

Mum says that I get real clingy when I sense that they are going away. Who wouldn't? No heaters at night, no one to play with or to have some interesting talks with! I know Becky won't be around because I heard her say that she is going with them. Unless Aunty Carla comes to stay…She is great fun! I'll have to wait and see…

I hung around mum this morning.

She decided to soak her toes in a bucket; she says it makes cutting toenails easier. The good part was that we were both sitting near the heater, though this made me quite thirsty, after a while. When she proceeded to cut her toenails, I decided to have a good drink of the water in the bucket. It tasted funny, probably because it was warm and because mum's toes had been soaking in it.

It did quench my thirst, though. I had a few more drinks. So, that's what people drink, several times a day: "warm beverages"!

Actually, I nearly brought the whole lot back up, ten minutes later. Warm beverages don't seem to agree with us cats, especially the toe-soaking kind!

Presently, I am lying on the bed in the main bedroom. Dad put mum's hot water bottle under the doona, right under me. I could feel that heavenly heat and I purred very loudly, to let him know how pleased I was.

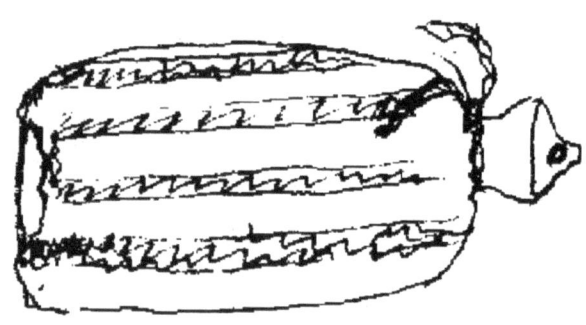

That's the kind of priority I feel is part of the Cats' Code of Rights'. More people should acquaint themselves with those. Well-done, dad!

Mum is sitting near me, on the bed. But wait! She has placed her icy feet near me, to warm them on my fur. Mum, take a leaf out of dad's book!

Tuesday, 13 July
COMINGS AND GOINGS IN OUR HOUSE

I have survived three days of misery! Mum and dad decided to lock me in the house, while away, in view of the possibility of other cats and dogs making their way in, through the cat door. Also, they don't like me being out at night because I like to hunt.

The only break came when Sara, James' mother, came to visit me twice. She let me run outside for a while but hunger soon drove me back in and she gave me my food. That was quite good. She talked to me and gave me some pats, which settled me right down. Night time was the worst; no heater and no one to talk to and get pats from.

Anyway, they eventually came back. The day after, dad left again, this time with his big back pack. Mum and Becky stayed home with me, though. Just as well. I am sure, I would have left home, otherwise!

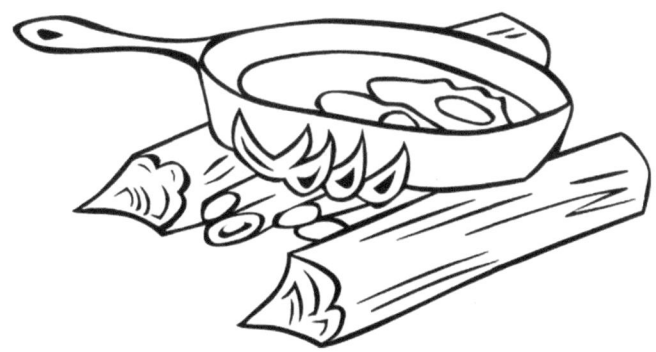

Saturday, 24 July **JUST LIKE A FILM STAR!**

Mum came home tonight, talking excitedly about a movie called "Shrek 2" she went to see with her friend Carla, my favourite cat sitter. What movie names they come up with! The character she talked about most was a cat called "Puss in Boots".

Apparently, he had a choking attack at a crucially strategic time in the movie. Mum said, just like I, when I have a fur ball. She thought that was funny! I personally would not find it funny at all. As well, he'd make these goggly eyes to get people in, before doing some serious damage. Just like Ginsey, she kept repeating. I thought she meant the "doing some serious damage" bit. She meant the "goggly eyes" bit. Ah well! Anyway, that proves that I easily could be in the movies, if I really wanted to.

Sunday, 25 July **BEDS, BEDS, BEDS!**

Today, mum and dad left early, wearing heavy boots, big back packs and carrying sticks. I didn't see them all day (sigh)!

I slept for a while, having access to all beds in all the bedrooms. I lied on the visitors' bed for a while, surveying our immediate neighbourhood for pesky intruders. All was clear. I then snacked on some leftover breakfast, hardly worth bothering, even though it was my second top-up (guilt offering, maybe?). Then, I jumped up on the antique table, where my drinking bowl is kept, a round glass container with some pretty, plastic water lilies in it. Mum always tells our visitors that I have mannerisms of a prince, snubbing my cat drinking bowl and using a receptacle intended for decoration. I say, I am a cat with breeding!

After that, it was time for my sleep on the big bed, in mum and dad's bedroom. Dad left his furry winter jumper on the bed, the dear. Mum calls it the "Man from Snowy River" jumper. I like kneading it and making a nest for myself.

I often dream of being a kitten again and suckling milk from my long-lost mumma, when I sleep on that jumper.

After a few hours of very peaceful sleep, the door opened and I ran to greet mum and dad. Instead, it was Becky. She came into the kitchen to use the microwave for some beauty treatment. I tried to look starved and put on my most endearing performance. In vain. After a while, she told me to get lost. It hurt!

When she left, I still followed her over to the cabin. I was allowed inside and proceeded to sniff around for some suspicious smells, such as the presence of other cats or dogs. When I could not find anything, I settled on her bed.

I slept there for a while, until she started using the horrid dust sucking machine. It gives me the creeps with its awful noise! It even started smoking, it's that old! I left in a hurry.

Later, mum and dad returned. Mum was limping. Dad started watching the footy and mum got onto the computer. She put a heat pack on her knee to soothe it. Poor mum!

After a while, she finally noticed that I was in distress too, due to what I thought was the "sticky flies syndrome". I was quite frantic because I could feel something on my back, where I could not reach it. "Not a sticky fly again, for heavens' sake!" I thought. Mum came and checked me out and could feel a lump. It turned out to be a tick instead! Mum then told dad, who got the cat first aid box out and got the tick out.

He is an expert tick remover, with fatal consequences for those nasty critters! Thanks mum and dad!

Finally, a breakthrough with the vexing sticky fly business! Mum has discovered the presence of sticky flies in the house! She swapped one; I saw its lifeless body lying on the ground, in the lounge room. What a sweet sight!

Since then, she has become very vigilant and has promptly discovered the erratic, alternate appearance and mysterious vanishing of another sticky fly. She told dad that she is determined to eradicate them from our home. Like I, she wants our home to be a place of peace, without sticky flies!

Is it not a little bit of a taste of heaven, when great minds think alike?

Back to the heater and the footy.

Saturday, 31 July **CAT BLISS**

I am lying on mum and dad's bed, snoozing and half listening to the noises around me. There is the noise of children somewhere in the distance, laughing, a dog barking on and off, music coming from the living room: dad's favourite singer called Bob Dylan, an old timer like dad. Dad is accompanying the music with his harmonica (mum says he is quite good at it) and mum is scrubbing the shower floor. It all is kind of peaceful because it's happening at a comfortable distance.

In a little while, I will do my round outside but for now I am going back to sleep...

Saturday, 14 August **CHECKMATE!**

Dad has gone to cards, I am home with mum. She spent some time in the study, playing on her computer. I quite like being in there (except... you know when not!) because she usually puts the heater on and I lie in front of it and feel cosy and warm. It is usually very quiet, only the tapping of the keyboard can be heard.

Mum then prepared her dinner and went and sat down to watch TV. That meant lap time for me. All was well until she decided to get up during the ads. I feel really put out by her restlessness; why can't she just stay seated in that blessed chair? So I did the next best thing to having lap time: I jumped up on the chair, enjoying the nice pre-heated spot. What did she do? She came back and pushed me off. I did not give in, without showing her my displeasure: trying to give her a little bite. She pulled her hand away very quickly and then pushed me off with a cushion, telling me how naughty I was! I opted for the best next thing: back to lap time!

Just as I was falling into a lovely deep sleep, what did she do? She got up again! The nuisance of it! So I just jumped up on the chair again. Ah! Lovely, comfy, warm armchair! But not for long; mum came back! And I was back down on the carpet. I sat there, near the heater, and just glared at her. Sometimes I don't like mum much!

This happened four times in all and I was pretty fed up in the end, actually from the start! It wasn't like we were playing a game. This was deadly serious – for both of us!

Being the wise, sensible and humble creature that I am, I finally settled on the cold armchair next to mum's and decided that she could get up and back sixty-six more times, for all I cared!

Eventually, mum went to bed. Before she did, she made a very bad mistake. She picked me up (I was livid about that too) and thought that she did me a great favour by placing me into the disputed chair. She needed to be taught a lesson and I gave her a nip on her hand. Was she annoyed! She told me something I can't repeat and then went to bed. I hate checkmate situations!

Bring back boys' night on the couch, anytime!

Tuesday, 24 August **A MISSED OPPORTUNITY**

I am sitting on the veranda table, in front of the large living room window. It is a late winter's morning, the air is filled with birdsong, humming and buzzing things and the lyrebird is busy practicing its repertoire of various bird songs, in preparation of courtship.

There is a delicate perfume in the air. Mum has put flowers on the table, multi-coloured flowering plants, whose petals emit a gorgeous scent. I think this décor is very becoming to a cat like me!

Now mum is looking at me and smiling. Why on earth isn't she fetching the camera?

Wednesday, 2 September
BETRAYAL AND MOVING ON TO A SECRET DIARY.

Something absolutely earth shattering has happened yesterday! Mum got hold of my diary and **she read it aloud to several family members** (who don't even like me. They hardly ever pat me and give me strange looks!)

How could she be this mean? I heard them all laugh very loud and some even had tears in their eyes, they laughed that hard! I feel deeply wounded and ridiculed; my dignity has been shred to tatters!

There is no other choice for me than to go underground, so to speak, with my diary writing. I am going to continue writing in my secret hiding place and no one will ever be able to laugh at me again! I will keep those writings away from intrusive eyes, in future. Good bye then, dear diary. I am moving on to another volume, **a secret volume!**

Your friend always,
Ginseng,
also called Ginsy.

(Photo of the real Ginsy)

To get in touch with Ginsy or author, please go to:
https://piahorangross.com

www.ingramcontent.com/pod-product-compliance
Lightning Source LLC
Chambersburg PA
CBHW042052290426
44110CB00001B/36